21 SECRETS OF MEDITATIONS SILICON VALLEY

Michael Gordon

TABLE OF CONTENTS

INTRODUCTION TO SILICON VALLEY

We have all heard about the "Silicon Valley" miracle. Not long ago, Silicon Valley found itself at the centre of the world, a job- and money-making machine fueled by the popularity of the Internet and technological innovation. Those days are a distant memory now. Now, the Center of the World has become a technological Rust Belt.

The streets, once throbbing with energy, are empty and quiet. Empty new buildings stand like bleached mausoleums in the sun with big, indiscreet "AVAILABLE" signs slapped on them. A full 20% of the valley's jobs have been lost since March 2001 and hi-tech jobs continued to be lost as companies downsize or outsource jobs to Asia. No one in the Valley can figure what to do to bring back the golden era.

However, most people not local to the area are unaware of the previous history of this area. The past 200 years have been tragic one of genocide, environmental destruction, greed, trickery, and exploitation. In 1776, at the time of their first contact with the Spanish explorers originally who were looking for gold, Santa Clara Valley was an untouched Eden with maybe 10,000 Ohlone Indians.

By 1830, the peaceful, basket-weaving peoples who had been living there for over 10,000 years had completely disappeared, killed off by epidemics and the mission system. In 1848, the land, originally part of Mexico, became part of United States. Americans, many of whom were failed gold-seekers from the mother lode, started to pour in and acquired Mexican cattle ranches, often through force and trickery. The rich alluvial soil-- some of the best in the world-- proved ideal for orchards.

The Valley during the spring was a canopy of white blossoms-- "The Valley of Heart's Delight." An orchard of another type grew around the seeds planted by William Hewlett, David Packard, Fred Terman, and other researchers at Stanford University. Today, Hewlett-Packard is one of the world's largest producers of computers and electronic measuring devices and equipment. The names of the branches of the tree are familiar: Stanford Industrial Park, Varian, Apple Computers, Intel, Yahoo, CISCO, Netscape, etc.

Creativity leads to innovation, and innovation leads to prosperity. Prosperity attracts restless, bright, often unscrupulous people, with often troubled and unhappy pasts, from all parts of the world. The old-time farmers sell their farms off for a king's ransom and move. The orchards were bulldozed to make room for subdivisions and industrial parks.

Beneath the high-tech sparkle laid a hidden underbelly of inequality, environmental devastation, and exploitation. A recent study of the Silicon Valley economy found that hourly wages of 75 percent of Silicon Valley workers were actually lower in 1996 than in 1989. Meanwhile, between 1992 and 1997, income for the top 20 percent has increased by 32 percent. The diverse workplace does not necessarily mean equality of opportunity. You see very few Hispanics or blacks in the hi-tech crystal palaces.

Silicon Valley has 29 Superfund sites--toxic sites slated for cleanup by the federal government. This is more than any other area in the country. High-tech manufacturing created 24 of the 29 sites; 18 are tied to the computer chip industry. At one time, the largest mercury mine in the U.S. was located in the New Alma den hills in the back of San Jose. Mercury, which is used to separate silver from base ore, seeps from this 100-year year old open sore and poisons the Guadalupe River and San Francisco Bay. The Hispanic hamlet of Alison lies partly on a landfill created by the dumping of asbestos-lined pipes in the 1950's by the Certainteed Corporation.

Will Silicon Valley ever regain its prosperity? Alternatively, it is like some new Atlantis being destroyed by its greed while its inhabitant scatter to the four winds. No one knows. Maybe, a large no strings attached investment, such as Leland Stanford's bequest that help found Stanford University, would help jump-start the economy. However, maybe, the problems faced by Silicon Valley are those, which cannot be solved by money alone. The entrepreneurial individualism, which has made the unnatural growth of the Valley possible, had, in the process, destroyed the social fabric that holds a society together.

The issues facing Silicon Valley today are social ones--pollution, growing income inequality, ethnic tension, unemployment, high housing costs, and a limited state budget. These problems had always been there, but were ignored and have worsened during the most rapid increase in wealth in history. Maybe, one day, the people of Silicon Valley and California will wake up and have the political will to spend the money needed to fix these problems. However, no one really knows

SILICON VALLEY - KEY INGREDIENTS FOR A TECH HUB

It started out with a bang. The great tech boom swept into San Francisco and Silicon Valley with a massive wave of investment and talented engineers. If a company could throw together a sock puppet and an HTML website they were sure to get millions. Unfortunately, the art of due diligence was tossed out the window like a soggy fast food carton as investment firms began to resemble forty-niners flocking to the gold rush more than prudent businessmen. Inevitably the bubble popped and the tech industry deflated. Fortunately, the foundation that was laid during the early days of the PC and throughout the tech boom left Silicon Valley uniquely capable of fostering innovation and supporting technology companies. Given the high growth associated with technology, other regions have begun to produce and foster high tech sectors. From New York media startups to Chicago's recent tech revival, what are the critical elements to supporting a vibrant technology industry? Here is an examination of some key characteristics that make Silicon Valley such a powerhouse.

Legal Foundation

One of the primary reasons that the Valley is such a tech magnet has to do with its legal environment. During the early sputtering days of innovation before the web 2.0 bubble, certain engineers in the valley decided to take chances. The area was known for research into early computing technology and certain employees developed innovative ideas that the larger companies were not completely willing to back. Shockley Semi Conductor laboratory offer a solid example. Initially founded to research the possibility of replacing germanium with silicon as the best material to build semiconductors, the company eventually gave up research due to assumed difficulties with manufacturing. As the company scaled back their efforts, several key engineers decided to take a risk and form their own company, Fairchild Semiconductor. That day Silicon Valley became Silicon Valley. The brazen risk taking approach has permeated the business culture of the area ever since. Given the increasing level of spin-offs and new ventures, legal firms in the area gained a wealth of expertise in forming, fostering and protecting new ventures. This legal expertise represents a key component to fostering the formation of new technology companies in the area to this day.

Venture Investment

The end of 1980 marked the beginning of the venture investment boom in Silicon Valley. As the local semiconductor industry took off, many players in the Sand Hill road area of Menlo Park began to look for opportunities to invest their new wealth. A couple of upstart entrepreneurs including Steve Jobs and Steve Wozniak had a little idea about selling kits for personal household computers. Despite the inherent risk of trying to sell computers for individual use, some investors took a chance on the nascent company called Apple. In 1980, Apple issued an initial public offering of 1.8 billion dollars. In the aftermath of this unprecedented success story both individuals and investment firms began to flock to the investment opportunities in the area. Over the years, these investment firms worked to develop a unique understanding of the needs and risks associated with financially fostering technology companies. A dynamic venture capital environment is a critical element for any would be technology hub. Without investment, tech sectors are almost guaranteed to fall behind other regions with more active investment firms.

Human Capital

As the chapter of the Great War closed, a ground swell of troops returned home with dreams of peace, families and success. Education was a primary focus. The GI bill provided an educational stimulus the likes of which had never existed before. Certain universities placed greater emphasis on their specialties to help provide a more useful education to the great numbers of applicants. Stanford, a school with a long history of computer science and engineering, began to buckle down and look for ways to enhance their stature in these fields. The Stanford Industrial park was an early attempt to bolster the technology prowess of the school. In a move to make use of available university owed land, Stanford decided to lease the land to local companies. One of the requirements set forth in the leasing decision was that each company must be in the technology industry. Companies from Hewlett-Packard to General Electric moved into the newly available space and began offering subsidies for their employees to attend graduate school at Stanford while they were working. This combination of educational and employment opportunities began to draw engineers to the region from all over the world. The web 2.0 bubble of the 1990's accelerated the pilgrimage of technology expertise to San Francisco and the greater Bay Area. Any ambitious engineer with an idea and a will could try their hand. Even after the boom, the sheer number of computer engineers in the greater Silicon Valley area is unrivaled. This wealth of available engineers represents the full spectrum of talent from 3rd rate hacks to world leading geniuses. For technology hubs, being able to effectively access your talent pool is almost as important as the availability of the talent itself. Given the supply of engineers,

Silicon Valley and San Francisco technical recruiting firms have sprung up to help match startups with the technical expertise required to realize their big ideas. Needless to say, human capital is probably the most critical factor for any region to become a center for technology companies.

Clout

The most intangible attribute, and probably the most universally acknowledged one, is the clout of Silicon Valley. Companies with roots in the area are actively competing with organizations on the cutting edge of technology. A corporate address in the Valley is almost like a stamp of approval. Between the venture firms priding themselves on due diligence and the top notch engineers, Silicon Valley has curb appeal. Clout is possibly the most difficult characteristic to achieve. For any aspiring technology hub, establishing legal protections, developing a venture friendly environment and courting engineering talent are the first major steps. With perseverance and a continued commitment to supporting the local technology industry a region can only hope to develop a level of clout capable of inspiring tech entrepreneurs for years to come. After all, inspiration is what puts the twinkle in the eyes of the next

Steve Jobs or Bill Gates to grace us with their grand ideas. Regardless of where the next big ideas spring up the characteristics the define Silicon Valley are sure to resonate in the next great technology Mecca.

STRUGGLING WITH DEPRESSION IN SILICON VALLEY

When you think of Silicon Valley, what's the first thing that comes to mind? The high-tech world? Apps, startup companies, or maybe even Facebook? The one thing linking those ideas together in Silicon Valley is the idea of wealth – fame and fortune seems to run rampant throughout the area, with bundles of money being thrown into the faces of young entrepreneurs. And by 'young,' we mean young. Most entrepreneurs behind Silicon Valley startups are in their early-to-mid twenties, and it can be safe to say, most of them are very intelligent.

This intelligence is exactly what can unfortunately lead to a big downfall, more often than not. In a recent study by Dr. Michael Freeman, a professor at UCSF, discovered that out of 242 new entrepreneurs surveyed, over 49% had a mental health condition. What's even more frightening? Depression was the top issue reported by those who struggled. Strangely enough, it wasn't because they were wealthy and had no idea what to do with their buckets and buckets of money. Most entrepreneurs who struggle with depression in Silicon Valley have to deal with it because they are afraid of failure.

Think about it – if you're in your early twenties, you decide to move to the tech hub of the country and start up your own business, in a world that seems to be running dry of totally fresh and new ideas, it might be a little intimidating. Chances are, you'll either have to put every penny of your life savings into that business, or borrow money from family, friends, or even the bank, putting you in debt instantly. And then…what happens if that business doesn't work out? There's a fairly common saying in

Silicon Valley, that 9 out of 10 new startups fail within the first year.

That's a pretty strong statement for someone looking to start their own business.

Unfortunately, many of these startups do fail, and people are starting to feel the pressure earlier and earlier in life. In more recent years, high schools in Palo Alto, CA have started introducing therapy to their students, simply because the surrounding environment pushes for success, etc., so much, that the pressure can become overwhelming. And, more and more young entrepreneurs are seeking professional help as well, as the suicide rate in Silicon Valley begins to slowly rise among entrepreneurs. Many CEO's of startup companies – even the successful ones – have stepped down, or taken a lesser role in their company due to their mental health and overall well being.

Depression and mental health are serious issues, especially when it comes to the pressures that come with owning/running a new company, or living in an area of the country that is surrounded by success, tech, etc. If you, or someone you know, might be struggling with a mental health issue of any kind, seeking professional help is always the best option. It's important to take care of yourself before your company, and that can include therapy sessions with someone who can help you learn how to manage the depression that's taken ahold of your mind. Silicon Valley may not be the perfect 'tech utopia' it seems to be, but it also doesn't have to be a terrifying dark cloud over California for entrepreneurs and those looking to live their dreams. Therapeutic help is out there for everyone, if you're willing to take the first step.

Causes & Effects of Depression

Sadness is a normal and common emotion that many people experience. Although sadness or the cause of the feeling may be unpleasant, sadness is a healthy emotion. However, depressive disorders differ from sadness in key ways. If feelings of sadness, lethargy, guilt, and similar emotions begin to impact normal daily living for two or more weeks without relief, and they begin to hinder an individual from performing daily tasks, this may indicate the presence of a depressive disorder.

Common symptoms of depression include feelings of emptiness, sadness, irritability, and possible somatic aches and pains. These symptoms must be severe enough to impact daily living. Three types of depressive disorders in adults include (but are not limited to) persistent depressive disorder, major depressive disorder, and premenstrual dysphoric disorder.

Major depressive disorder: Major depressive disorder is characterized by episodes of sadness, lack of energy or motivation, loss of enthusiasm or happiness, sudden changes in weight related to changes in appetite, persistent feelings of hopelessness, changes in sleeping patterns, inability to focus, and/or suicidal tendencies that last for at least two weeks.

Persistent depressive disorder: Formerly known as dysthymia, this disorder is characterized by low-level depression that is very difficult to cope with. This disorder must last at least two years before diagnosis. Symptoms include low energy, low self-esteem, poor concentration, appetite disturbances, and/or feelings of hopelessness. However, the symptoms are usually constant and can last longer, yet are less severe.

Premenstrual dysphoric disorder: This condition also has almost the same symptoms as major depressive disorder. However, this type of depressive disorder is linked to the female menstrual cycle, yet symptoms are more severe than regular premenstrual emotions. Irritability, anxiety, mood swings, dysphoria, and depression before the cycle begins are among the common symptoms.

All depressive disorders greatly affect an individual's life in a negative manner. Depression is a disorder that will worsen over time without treatment, so many people do not seek help until depression becomes severe.

On the bright side, depressive disorders can be treated through therapy and support. With immediate help, an individual can have the opportunity to live a happier, normal life.

Statistics

About 6.7% of U.S. citizens have depression. In the United States, this means that 14.8 million individuals are struggling with this disorder. Based on studies made by the National Institute of Mental Health, depression is often first diagnosed in young adults, ages 18 to 25. An increase of depression cases is seen again at age 50. Women are more likely to develop this condition and seek help for this condition than men. Women are three times more likely to report major depressive disorder to a mental health clinician.

Causes and Risk Factors for Depressive Disorders

Depression can be influenced by a number of risk factors, including the following:

Genetic: Heredity plays a significant role in the development of depression. Studies by the American Psychiatric Association show that individuals with a family history of depressive disorders have 400% greater risk of developing depression than do individuals whose family members have not struggled with depression.

Environmental: Environmental influences and current experiences can trigger a depressive disorder. Traumatic events, stress, and life's difficulties may trigger this condition. Childhood traumatic experiences such as bullying, abuse, poverty, or family violence can also contribute to depressive disorders. If the environment that surrounds an individual is negative or unsupportive, the risk of depression rises.

Risk Factors:

Alcoholism and substance use or abuse

Traumatic experiences

Women reportedly have higher rates of depression than men

Young adults ages 18 to 29 have higher risk of depression

Negative thoughts

Loss or death of a loved one

A history of depressive disorders in the family

Signs and Symptoms of Depressive Disorders

Like other mental health disorders, depression symptoms can vary from case to case. Personality and history of an individual can determine the symptoms that he or she will show. Common symptoms include the following:

Behavioral symptoms:

Ignoring regular and leisure activities

Neglect in school or work responsibilities

Slowed movement and talking

Episodes of crying or weeping

Easily irritated and angered

Agitated and anxious

Physical symptoms:

Significant change in weight

Change in eating habits

Somatic (body) pains like stomachache or headache

Excessive sleepiness or fatigue

Unusual sleeping habits

Cognitive symptoms:

Slow thought process

Easily distracted

Inability to focus or concentrate

Inability to make decisions

Thoughts of giving up, running away, or dying

Psychosocial symptoms:

Irritability

Sadness, guilt, or shame

Being withdrawn

Suicidal tendencies

If you feel that you are in crisis, or are having thoughts about hurting yourself or others, please call 9-1-1 or go to the nearest emergency room immediately.

Effects of Depressive Disorders

If an individual with a depressive disorder is not given help, it can lead to dangerous and traumatic consequences such as the following:

Loss of job and income

Inability to perform at work or school

Family and relationship conflicts

Disturbed sleeping patterns that lead to fatigue

Being withdrawn and isolated from others

Dangerous or risky actions

Substance use and abuse

Self-inflicted injuries

Suicidal tendencies

Suicidal ideation

Co-Occurring Disorders

Depressive disorders may co-occur with the following mental health conditions:

Anxiety disorder

Eating disorder

Obsessive-compulsive disorder (OCD)

Posttraumatic stress disorder (PTSD)

Substance use disorder

Tactics to manage your mental health

If the above is still too abstract or just plain nonsense, here are other ways I've found that help me manage my mental health.

1) Exercise the body

Seriously. There is scientific proof that exercising your body will help minimize stress and depression levels. I challenge myself to at least 1 hour a day of exercise, either at the gym, playing volleyball, biking, or a 15 minute walk around the park. If you were like me when I first started TINT, and you believe exercising won't be as "effective" as hammering out emails, you're wrong. Taking care of your body will ease your mind so that you can be that much more creative or efficient in your tasks.

2) Exercise the Mind

Your brain acts just like a muscle, and needs exercise. The two ways I exercise my mind is through meditation and reading.

I now meditate 15 minutes a day — I used the meditation app Headspace to help me develop my practice. You might fall asleep the first few times– that's normal. After you get through the learning curve, you will see how much it can calm your racing mind to be the most effective it can be. Sometimes, I'll listen to guided meditations on the bus, or relaxing peaceful music during work. It works wonders.

WHAT IS MEDITATION?

These are common questions that people began to learn about meditation. In the West, the word meditation means a concentrated state of mind in serious reflection. The Latin root of the word meditation, mederi, means "to heal". So "What is meditation?" You should not complicate the answer, simply understood: Meditation is an approach that anyone can use to help them cope with medical problems, stress, and anxiety by way of thought, contemplation, and reflection.

Origin

Finding the origin of meditation may be quite difficult. Meditation is deep rooted in Asia, and countries like China, India and Japan are practicing it for thousands of years. Tribes in South India had developed Tantric Meditation about 15 thousand years back. Tantric meditation was in common use those days. So, we can put forward that concept of meditation emerged from Asia and took various forms in all over the world. Other views about the origin of meditation claims that it originated from the human being's curiosity for the purpose of men, purpose of the universe and to find God by looking inside the self to realize the nature and its existence.

Historical Perspectives

All historians have consensus over the points that, meditation has evolved during unknown ancient times and that; it was not practiced in such a way in which it is practiced today. Taoists started practicing meditation during 500 to 600 BC. Buddhists also started using meditation in the same era. In history, Buddha is one of the greatest promoters of meditation. He was the one to teach meditation in Asia during 500 BC. Buddha has introduced the basic forms of meditation, and all the world adapted and transformed these meditation techniques according to their needs and purposes. Important point to note here is that, Eastern countries were the origin of meditation and getting relief through various meditation techniques. West had adapted this culture from East. During 20th century, Western researchers conducted researches on meditation and came to know about its physical and psychological benefits. Since then, they are using meditation as a wide spread practice in their culture. Western population widely practiced meditation for peace of mind and to get relief from daily life stresses. Nowadays, a downfall has been observed in practices of meditation, and reason is lack of time.

Many years ago meditation was considered something just not meant for modern people, but now it has become very popular with all types of people. Published scientific and medical evidence has proved its benefits.

Meditation encompasses a variety of practices that are somewhat different, while holding to the basic principles of consideration and quiet thought to bring about a state of rumination. Various types of meditation that are recognized include prayer, Zen, Taoist, mindfulness, and Buddhist. Some methods of meditation may require the body being absolutely still or to be moved with controlled deliberation, while other types allow for free movement of the body. While the methods are different, the end goal of all types of meditation lead to a mind that is quieted and free from stress by the use of quiet contemplation and reflection.

Most techniques called meditation include these components:

1. You sit or lie in a relaxed position.
2. You breathe regularly. You breathe in deep enough to get enough oxygen. When you breathe out, you relax your muscles so that your lungs are well emptied, but without straining.
3. You stop thinking about everyday problems and matters.
4. You concentrate your thoughts upon some sound, some word you repeat, some image, some abstract concept or some feeling. Your whole attention should be pointed at the object you have chosen to concentrate upon.
5. If some foreign thoughts creep in, you just stop this foreign thought, and go back to the object of meditation.

The different meditation techniques differ according to the degree of concentration, and how foreign thoughts are handled. By some techniques, the objective is to concentrate so intensely that no foreign thoughts occur at all.

In other techniques, the concentration is more relaxed so that foreign thoughts easily pop up. When these foreign thoughts are discovered, one stops these and goes back to the pure meditation in a relaxed manner. Thoughts coming up, will often be about things you have forgotten or suppressed, and allow you to rediscover hidden memory material. This rediscovery will have a psychotherapeutic effect.

THE EFFECTS OF MEDITATION

Meditation has the following effects:

1. Meditation will give you rest and recreation.
2. You learn to relax.
3. You learn to concentrate better on problem solving.
4. Meditation often has a good effect upon the blood pressure.
5. Meditation has beneficial effects upon inner body processes, like circulation, respiration and digestion.
6. Regular meditation will have a psychotherapeutically effect.
7. Regular meditation will facilitate the immune system.
8. Meditation is usually pleacent.

THE DIFFERENCE BETWEEN HYPNOSIS AND MEDITATION

Hypnosis may have some of the same relaxing and psychotherapeutic effects as meditation. However, when you meditate you are in control yourself; by hypnosis you let some other person or some mechanical device control you. Also hypnosis will not have a training effect upon the ability to concentrate.

A SIMPLE FORM OF MEDITATION

Here is a simple form of meditation:

1. Sit in a good chair in a comfortable position.
2. Relax all your muscles as well as you can.
3. Stop thinking about anything, or at least try not to think about anything.
4. Breath out, relaxing all the muscles in your breathing apparatus.
5. Repeat the following in 10 - 20 minutes:
   - Breath in so deep that you feel you get enough oxygen.

- Breath out, relaxing your chest and diaphragm completely.
- Every time you breathe out, think the word "one" or another simple word inside yourself. You should think the word in a prolonged manner, and so that you hear it inside you, but you should try to avoid using your mouth or voice.

6. If foreign thoughts come in, just stop these thoughts in a relaxed manner, and keep on concentrating upon the breathing and the word you repeat.

As you proceed through this meditation, you should feel steadily more relaxed in your mind and body, feel that you breathe steadily more effectively, and that the blood circulation throughout your body gets more efficient. You may also feel an increasing mental pleasure throughout the meditation.

THE SECRETS OF MEDITATION IN SILICON VALLEY

Depression is a clinical disease that engulfs the normal self of a person when the stress levels are high, and one doesn't feel normal about their lives. There may be several reasons for depression like professional strain, problems in the family or a serious issue with an important aspect of one's life. It can be cured with the help of medicines, but the best way to get over it is meditation and Yoga. Meditation involves sitting in solidarity and thus reducing the levels of stress by performing relevant activities. There are ways that meditation can normalize a brain and get rid of depression. They may be categorized as follows -

The deactivation of the depression areas in the brain - When a person meditates, the brain goes into a slumber. The areas that control the anxiety and stress levels in the brain gets deactivated automatically as people do not tend to think of their worries while meditating. The practice of such deactivation on a daily basis lets the depression reduce completely.

Helping the mind to think about the present - There are people who tend to think about the past incidents of their lives which were disturbing. The disturbing memories sometimes increase the stress levels and making people depressed. There is a similar effect on those who think about their future and what it holds for them. This therapy calms the mind and thus letting people think of the present and not fret about what has happened or what will happen.

Helps in reacting to situations - Different people have their perspectives to look at the world and the ways to react to each incident that takes place. There are people who tend to worry and get depressed about each and everything around them. As it helps in soothing the conditions of the mind and bringing about patience in their lives, people tend to react to different situations with ease depending on its seriousness and how it affects their lives. People no longer panic while handling serious situations and sort them out with ease.

Brings about the feeling of being content - People at times feel the need for everything in their lives. They may not be able to afford it, and thus the feeling of depression sets it. It helps in soothing the mind and being content with whatever they have. People tend to feel better about their lives and what they have when their minds are content. The stress levels thus reduce naturally and bring about a change in one's body.

Yoga is an ancient Indian practice that disciplines the mind and body through a series of poses known as asanas. Each asana is held for a period of time with the aim of strengthening the mind as well as the body, due to the concentration required to hold the pose. Yoga is also about connecting with yourself by gaining an insight into your inner self. When depression strikes, it is said that the person has lost the connection to themselves. Devotees of yoga claim that it has amazing inner healing powers and because of this, yogis (those who practice yoga) are able to deal with depression and other mental health problems better than those who do not practice the discipline.

Studies have found that yoga is helpful in cases of depression, anxiety, stress, bipolar conditions and other mental health problems. In the UK, yoga is being offered as a form of alternative therapy on the NHS. In New York, yoga is offered as a treatment by psychiatrists to their patients.

Because of the side effects of many mental health drugs, yoga is increasingly being seen as a popular alternative to harsh drugs. For example, yoga is deemed an effective treatment for those suffering from schizophrenia. Yoga works to calm the body and hence the mind due to the steady and controlled breathing that is required in order to complete the postures.

Fans of yoga have found that they are able to transfer this skill to other areas of their life, particularly when they are feeling anxious because they are able to slow down their breathing and also their heart rate.

Meditation is one of the practices of yoga, and involves using controlled breathing together with inner reflection and focusing on an object or a particular set of thoughts. Meditation that is geared towards helping mental health problems involves dealing with negative thoughts and feelings which can affect a person's confidence and self-esteem.

Meditation is used by monks as part of their daily ritual to instill calmness and control within the body. They also use meditation as a means to reach within themselves and attain inner peace and harmony, so that they are essentially at one with themselves. This notion of being completely at one with yourself is seen as one of the keys to being truly happy from within.

Meditation is an excellent way to help calm and focus the mind as well as deal with negativity and replace them with positive thoughts and a happier mindset. Research has found meditation to be highly effective in treating depression and preventing severe bouts of depression from returning.

One of the many benefits of meditation is that those people who meditate regularly have an exceptional ability to handle stressful situations with a calm and clear mind. Anyone can experience the life enhancing qualities that meditation can bring, simply by playing meditation CDs. These are widely available online and can be used to help a number of conditions from weight loss to depression and treating anxiety and stress.

Yoga and meditation go hand in hand, and aside from their numerous health benefits, they are a viable alternative to drugs for those people who suffer from depression and other mental health problems.

Meditation is an up and coming treatment to help alleviate one of the biggest problems faced by many people today: an overactive mind. Though being busy is typically a good thing, dealing with racing thoughts on a daily basis can often to lead to stress and tension. When you are overloaded in that way, you can suffer from all sorts of physical ailments, such as high blood pressure, poor rest and anxiety. With that in mind, psychologists are looking to help people deal with this mind stress. In lieu of medications, psychologists are using a natural treatment in the form of meditation.

When people are suffering from anxiety, anger, or depression, they just need to slow down. Their thoughts are often racing and they never give their body or their mind a chance to calm down and take account of the things around them. One of the best ways to stop these issues is by giving the mind a break. For this, psychologists are choosing meditation as their primary means of treatment.

So what are the positive effects of meditation, at least in terms of cooling the mind? Individuals are able to stay calm and balanced through a multitude of situations. When meditation is used, the mind slows down and individuals are able to actually think their way through different circumstances. What this creates is a scenario where individuals are able to fight off thoughts of depression and are able to quell the devastating effects of anxiety. Meditation has been known to lead to feelings of happiness and vitality.

Different types of meditation has been around for centuries. The reason it has been able to sustain over the years has everything to do with the intrinsic ability of individuals to stay calm. When you use this ancient remedy, you are able to raise your own intuition and this brings about more self-confidence. With so many positive thoughts flowing and the mind slowing down all of the negative thought processes, it is no wonder why so many psychologists are using meditation to help counteract common mental issues.

So what types of meditation are most beneficial for those with a host of different mental conditions?

Guided meditation is one of the best ways to calm the mind. This is when people use imagery to get to a place that's more soothing and more relaxing. They work to relieve stress by replacing poor thoughts with nice thoughts.

Qi Gong comes from China and is considered a top form of meditation for calming the mind. It includes breathing exercises, as well as physical movement and relaxation.

Mantra meditation is another type of relaxation where you repeat a word over and over to achieve a state of relaxation. Each of these is right for certain types of people, and they all attempt to remove negative thoughts, while replacing them with happy, positive thoughts.

The benefits of meditation are profound because they bring peace to both the body and the mind. With so many diseases and conditions being related to stress, it is absolutely essential that individuals do everything in their power to put stress to rest. If the mind is never allowed to rest and relax, individuals have little chance of finding real inner peace. Having a clear, rested self makes sleeping much easier and it brings about better overall health, according to psychologists.

Depression can also be looked at a state or a 'condition' that could be temporary. The person suffering is unable to get out of the trap of thinking about something in the past and is unable to see much positive in the present. This is depression. It is a state of the body and the mind. Sometimes the person has gone through many traumas and has experienced many losses and is angry with many people. Despite keeping themselves busy, such people experience a low grade depressive state that they cannot explain or understand. This happens because 'understanding' occurs at a conscious level. At the subconscious or unconscious level, the body and the mind still carry the burden of the unpleasant experiences. People who have stiff upper lip will say- 'I do not know why I am suffering. But life has to go on'. This statement

comes from the conscious (understanding) part of the mind. Unfortunately, suffering is a feeling and it is 'unconscious'. How can you treat a 'feeling' with logic? It is not possible. It is not possible because logic and feeling are two different parameters. You cannot measure one against the other.

Meditation, like hypnosis, works at an unconscious level. The interesting part is that meditation also affects our conscious mind.

So whatever unconscious changes are brought about in the mind, they affect the logical and conscious part of our mind too. This is the principal basis on which meditation helps in a depressed state.

Many times people who are depressed about the past are also anxious about the future. Anxiety is a state of arousal or over-stimulation of the nervous system. It is this arousal state that causes increased secretion of cortisol- a stress hormone. So depressed people tend to have an increased stress in their bodies and not less stress. They are slow because they reach a state of physical and mental exhaustion Even from common sense point of view, the treatment for exhaustion is rest. In the case of the emotional and nervous exhaustion, rest of the mind is the treatment of choice. How is our mind rested? Not with sleep, but it rests with meditation.

Though in old literature, meditation and hypnosis have been contraindicated in depression, I have used both, in helping patients with depression. (For more information you can read the article - Meditation Can Make You Emotionally Distressed) Meditation and antidepressants have opposite effects on the nervous system. The former releases emotions locked up in the body, the latter block the emotions in the body.

Meditation can be helpful in clearing up the emotional distress that one is experiencing with depression. If you want to use meditation as a drug, you can. Just like the dosage of a drug is increased or decreased, depending on need, the time spent on meditation can be increased or decreased and the variable effects will be experienced.

In the first instance, as you start meditation, do not spend more than five minutes doing it daily. Sick to five minutes of meditation and do not do more than five minutes. Initially you will feel better.

This effect would last for a few days. Then you will start to feel depressed or angry. If you can handle the feeling that comes, carry on doing the meditation for five minutes daily. If you cannot handle it, stop doing meditation for two or three days. Within 48 to72 hours of you stopping the meditation, you will feel better. As soon as that happens, start doing the meditation again for five minutes daily. Again, you may feel depressed or angry after a few days. Again stop doing meditation for a few days till you start to feel better. Again start meditation daily for five minutes daily.

As time goes on, your body will become used to relaxing with five minutes of meditation. If you do not feel angry or low for two weeks at a stretch as you continue meditation, it is time to make further progress. Your body is now ready to relax more. You can then increase the meditation to seven minutes a day. The same steps, as above, have to be followed till you have two weeks of 'good period'. Then increase the meditation to ten minutes a day.

Remember that the effects of meditation and medication are in the opposite direction. Meditation relaxes by releasing emotions, meditation numbs the emotions, so you feel nothing. So if you come off medication quickly and start meditation to cure yourself, you will go into depression fast. Coming off antidepressant medication has the same effect on the body as starting to meditate. The body tends to come back into its original emotional state.

Medication vs. Meditation - Which Method Is Better for Depression?

Depression is a potentially life-threatening mood disorder and is also known as a silent killer that has been overlooked for years. If affects 1 in 6 persons in the United States, or approximately 17.6 million Americans each year. As many as two thirds of people with depression do not realize that they have a treatable illness and do not seek treatment.

For those who do seek treatment and are willing to look for help, most of them turn to the only treatment they know, medication in the form of anti-depressants. People may not realize it but there is another alternative instead of just medicine which in my personal opinion is like putting a 'band-aid 'on the issue.

Think about this for a moment. Depression is not something that happens overnight. Isn't depression simply layers and layers of sadness, unhappiness, emotional pain that has been built up over time? If you agree, wouldn't it make sense then that by taking medication, all that really does is externally numbs a person. So what happens next? You would have to keep increasing the dosage therefore increasing their side effects. In my opinion the risk and side effects with medication outweighs the benefits in the long run.

How do I know? I've witnessed countless people with many emotional problems heal naturally once they understand how the simple method of meditation can help. Don't get me wrong, I am not against medication but I do believe and have witnessed the short term effects and dangerous side effects it causes.

I know people who have had extreme cases of depression transform their life completely when given the proper meditation techniques. You see, this transformation isn't short term nor does it have any negative side effects. In fact these depressed people have such a positive change that it touches everyone around them, creating a healthy and happy ripple effect for many others as well.

True meditation is not about calming the mind, sitting in silence, and finding peace alone. It's about observation of the mind and body and pinpointing exactly where the source of the problem is. Once the source is found, then problems no longer repeat. Can you imagine family and friends no longer riding on the emotional roller coaster? What would life be like for everyone?

Meditation truly is the only way I know for sure that can successfully help someone recover from depression and many other emotional pains they may be going through. Why? Simply because all the answers are within each person. When a person meditates they see and experience the true answer themselves. Its real, it's the truth and its right before their eyes. It's nothing read, or written, or taken in from outside themselves. Meditation is a practice that does require guidance and help from an experienced practitioner or teacher. Results are immediate with increasing benefits day by day.

Truly, what does a person have to lose? Except for the negative, lifeless, depressing mood that could lead to dangerous actions if not treated. I admit I have been touched by meditation in ways I cannot describe. I have seen the miracles that result from this method and now dedicate a part of my life to sharing the amazing benefits so that anyone and everyone can live a happier and healthier life.

Scientific Basis of Meditation - How Science Proves The Effectiveness of Meditation

When people hear the term meditation, they instantly connect it with archaic spiritual and pseudoscientific practices,but the truth remains that not only meditation has immense scientifically proved benefits but it also based on the principles of science. Contrary to the common belief that meditation is all about sitting still, there are actually numerous ways to meditate even on the go.

A lot of the methods involve meditation in some sort of motion, but does this really have a scientific base or are we just romanticizing a concept based on more of a placebo effect? While some continue to negate the link, here's taking a look at how science proves the healing power of meditation.

Effect of Meditation on Brain Waves, and consequently on the state of the mind- It is already established that brain uses electromagnetic waves to function. There are different types of brain waves- the Beta Wave that are responsible for logical thinking, awareness, the Alpha Wave concerned with meditation, relaxation, the Theta wave concerned with an out-of-the body experience or daydreaming. A study testing the efficacy of Sahaja Yoga confirmed that during the test phase the meditators experienced pre-dominant Alpha waves.

Meditation Increases Concentration Span- Well this is actually no rocket science. In today's era where the maximum attention span is of 6 seconds, it is very difficult to concentrate on anything for long. A study published in PLOS Biology suggests that three months of consistent meditation can train the brain to increase the attention span. The director of the Center for Mind and Brain at the California University spoke in context of the study and called it neuroscience evidence' that changes the working of the brain through meditation.

Meditation can help lower blood pressure- In a study conducted on 200 heart patients, it was found that patients who meditated on a regular scale had over the time shown a decrease in the blood pressure. It is to be noted that all of these patients had heart conditions. Those who meditated were also disease free comparatively than those who did not meditate. It was also found that meditation helps to reduce the systolic blood pressure by an average of five millimeters of mercury.

Meditation increases the reasoning power- When a person meditates, their minds are in a state of calm. The basic principle of meditation is to induce calm by getting rid of the random thoughts that charge throughout the mind, and one which makes reasoning difficult by clouding it with other unrelated thoughts. A research conducted at UCLA using MRI showed that among the group of subjects, certain areas of the brain of those who meditated regularly were larger. Basically these areas were the ones associated with emotions, which is why meditation is also recommended to those with emotionally triggered disorders. Since meditation gives the power to control the emotions, it indirectly also makes a person's ability to reason out better.

Meditation builds up a healthier brain- Ask someone who meditates on a regular basis and have been doing so for years, they will tell you how they do not need a lot of sleep or tons of caffeine to charge their minds and bodies. Those who meditate condition their brains over a period of time to become healthier. Getting rid of negative thoughts, improving concentration power and attention span, and the ability to think and reason out better are all important requirements of a healthy brain and hence a healthy body. And studies conducted on a group of meditators proved that meditation does indeed help in improving the overall health of the brain.

Meditation reduces anxiety, stress, and depression- Probably a no-brainer since meditation is highly recommended for anyone going through or has stress and depression issues. According to a study published in Psychosomatic Medicine in 2009, the effects of meditation on stress and depression was calculated and it was established that meditation does indeed help to both reduce the level of stress and anxiety, and help with depression while at the same time it empowers the meditator to fight against these, thus working as a preventive measure as well.

The concept is still in its infancy and every day a number of studies and researches are being conducted to understand the link better and to scientifically quantify or deny meditation which has a therapeutic effect. Having said that, meditation does indeed work wonders for our overall mental and physical health, from attaining peace of mind to control over emotions.

While we are yet to prove the concept of meditation through scientific laws and formulas, it is safe to say that the benefits of meditation have already been established as per studies and experiments. For anyone looking to overcome emotional problems and mental disorders, meditation does make it a lot easier, and this is why even doctors strongly recommend this.

Below are other secret why daily meditation can benefit your hectic life:

Stress Reduction

Practicing meditation aids in lowering our stress levels by training us to shift from the fears that can pester us through-out our lives. Meditating 15-30 minutes a day helps calm the psyche and concentrating on the present-day ensures we gain inner tranquility.

Daily Meditation benefits your health

Frequent studies on meditation have shown that it benefits your health. Though, this does not mean that meditation will promise you decent health. What I mean is, if your mind is in constant stress and anxiety it will lower your body's resistance to illness. For example if you mind is always in inner chaos it will likely cause heart disease and other ailments. With frequent meditation it can give you inner peace which can aid in eluding numerous stress linked disorders. It has also been said that meditation has also been shown to stop pain connected with many ailments.

Meditation helps to Control Your Thoughts

Mankind is a remarkable animal. Science has done so much to help us rid the world of dangerous diseases, explored the world and universe, and made the world a much better place for the ordinary individual to live in. Though, the world is a better place now for the majority of us, the question is how do we master our own psyche? What I mean is do you often find yourself thinking negative thoughts? How do you deal with it? Meditation instills that it is possible to govern your thoughts. With the help of meditation you can bring your disorderly psyche under control. Controlling your negative thoughts through meditation will help produce a tranquil mind which permits you to accomplish what you want to in your existence.

Bliss and Harmony of Awareness

With the help of meditation it can take us to the foundation of contentment. When we have no harmony of awareness we are continually confronted by negative thoughts, bliss will continue to be evasive. If we can meditate with a tranquil awareness, it will help us to discover an unanticipated source of bliss inside our own ego. Daily meditation demonstrates to us that bliss is not reliant on just our external surroundings, but also on our internal approach as well.

Furthermore on the secrets of meditation in Silicon Valley

1. Brain & Moods

Meditation is like multivitamins for your brain. Good to take it every day.

Mindfulness practices decreases depression

In a study conducted at five middle schools in Belgium, involving about 400 students (13 ~ 20 years old), Professor Filip Raes concludes that "students who follow an in-class mindfulness program report reduced indications of depression, anxiety and stress up to six months later. Moreover, these students were less likely to develop pronounced depression-like symptoms."

Another study, from the University of California, made with patients with past depression, concluded that mindfulness meditation decreases ruminative thinking and dysfunctional beliefs.

Yet another concludes that mindfulness meditation may be effective to treat depression to a similar degree as antidepressant drug therapy".

ork

Mindfulness meditation helps treat depression in mothers to be

High-risk pregnant women who participated in a ten-week mindfulness yoga training saw significant reductions in depressive symptoms, according to a University of Michigan Health System pilot feasibility study. The mothers-to-be also showed more intense bonding to their babies in the womb. The findings were published in Complementary Therapies in Clinical Practice.

Meditation practices help regulate mood and anxiety disorders

This is also the conclusion of over 20 randomized controlled studies taken from PubMed, PsycInfo, and the Cochrane Databases, involving the techniques of Meditation, Meditative Prayer, Yoga, Relaxation Response. Another research concludes that mindfulness meditation may be effective to treat anxiety to a similar degree as antidepressant drug therapy.

Meditation was found to be as effective to treat anxiety and depression as antidepressant drug...

Meditation reduces stress and anxiety in general

A study from the University of Wisconsin-Madison indicates that the practice of "Open Monitoring Meditation" (such as Vipassana), reduces the grey-matter density in areas of the brain related with anxiety and stress. Meditators were more able to "attend moment-to-moment to the stream of stimuli to which they are exposed and less likely to 'get stuck' on any one stimulus. "

"Open Monitoring Meditation" involves non-reactively monitoring the content of experience from moment-to-moment, primarily as a means to recognize the nature of emotional and cognitive patterns.

Meditation helps reduce symptoms of panic disorder

In a research published in the American Journal of Psychiatry, 22 patients diagnosed with anxiety disorder or panic disorder were submitted to 3 months meditation and relaxation training. As a result, for 20 of those patients the effects of panic and anxiety had reduced substantially, and the changes were maintained at follow-up.

Meditation increases grey matter concentration in the brain

A group of Harvard neuroscientists ran an experiment where 16 people were submitted to an eight-week mindfulness course, using guided meditations and integration of mindfulness into everyday activities. The results were reported by Sara Lazar, PhD. At the end of it, MRI scans show that the grey matter concentration increases in areas of the brain involved in learning and memory, regulating emotions, sense of self, and having perspective.

What meditation does to your brain?

Meditation acutely improves psychomotor vigilance, and may

decrease sleep need

Meditation provides at least a short-term performance improvement even in novice meditators. In long term meditators, multiple hours spent in meditation are associated with a significant decrease in total sleep time when compared with age and sex matched controls who did not meditate. Whether meditation can actually replace a portion of sleep or pay-off sleep debt is under further investigation.

Long-term meditation enhances the ability to generate gamma waves in the brain

In a study with Tibetan Buddhist monks, conducted by neuroscientist Richard Davidson of the University of Wisconsin, it was found that novice meditators "showed a slight increase in gamma activity, but most monks showed extremely large increases of a sort that has never been reported before in the neuroscience literature".

Mind & Performance

Meditation improves information processing and decision-making

long-term meditators have larger amounts of gyrification ("folding" of the cortex, which may allow the brain to process information faster) than people who do not meditate. Scientists suspect that gyrification is responsible for making the brain better at processing information, making decisions, forming memories and improving attention.

meditation reduces pain

Meditation relieves pain better than morphine. In an experiment conducted by Wake Forest Baptist Medical Centre, 15 healthy volunteers, who were new to meditation, attended four 20-minute classes to learn meditation, focusing on the breath. Both before and after meditation training, study participants' brain activity was examined using ASL MRI, while pain was inflicted in them by using heat.

This is the first study to show that only a little over an hour of meditation training can dramatically reduce both the experience of pain and pain-related brain activation. (…) We found a big effect – about a 40 percent reduction in pain intensity and a 57 per reduction in pain unpleasantness. Meditation produced a greater reduction in pain than even morphine or other pain-relieving drugs, which typically reduce pain ratings by about 25 percent."

In a study made with 50 adult ADHD patients, the group that was submitted to MBCT (Mindfulness-based cognitive therapy) demonstrated reduced hyperactivity, reduced impulsivity and increased "act-with-awareness" skill, contributing to an overall improvement in inattention symptoms.

Meditation increases the ability to keep focus in spite of distractions

A study from Emory University, Atlanta, demonstrated that participants with more meditation experience exhibit increased connectivity within the brain networks controlling attention. These neural relationships may be involved in the development of cognitive skills, such as maintaining attention and disengaging from distraction. Moreover, the benefits of the practice were observed also in normal state of consciousness during the day, which speaks to the transference of cognitive abilities "off the cushion" into daily life.

The meditation practice examined was focusing the attention on the breath.

Meditation improves learning, memory and self-awareness

Long-term practice of meditation increases grey-matter density in the areas of the brain associated with learning, memory, self-awareness, compassion, and introspection.

Mindfulness meditation improves rapid memory recall

Meditation improves your mood and psychological well-being

Meditation prevents you from falling in the trap of multitasking too often

Multitasking is not only a dangerous productivity myth, but it's also a source of stress. "Changing gears" between activities is costly for the brain, and induces feelings of distraction and dissatisfaction from the work being done.

In a research conducted by the University of Washington and University of Arizona, Human Resource personnel were given 8 weeks of training in either mindfulness meditation or body relaxation techniques, and were given a stressful multitasking test both before and after training. The group of staff that had practiced meditation reported lower levels of stress and showed better memory for the tasks they had performed; they also switched tasks less often and remained focused on tasks longer.

Meditation helps us allocate limited brain resources

When the brain is presented two targets to pay attention to, and they right after one another (half a second difference), the second one is often not seen. This is called "attentional-blink".

In an experiment conducted by the University of California, a stream of random letters was shown in a computer screen, in rapid succession. In each session, one or two numbers or blank screens would appear in the middle, and participants were later asked, immediately after the stream ended, to type the numbers they saw. They were also asked whether they thought a blank screen was shown or not.

Subjects that had undergone 3 months of intense Vipassana Meditation were found to have a better control over the distribution of attention and perception resources. They showed less allocation of brain-resource for each letter shown, which resulted in reduction in "attentional-blink" size.

Meditation improves visuospatial processing and working memory

Research has shown that even after only four sessions of mindfulness meditation training, participants had significantly improved visuospatial processing, working memory, and executive functioning.

Meditation prepares you to deal with stressful events

A study from All India Institute of Medical Sciences, conducted with 32 adults that had never practiced meditation before, showed that if meditation is practiced before a stressful event, the adverse effects of stress were lessened.

Meditation increases awareness of your unconscious mind

A study by researchers from the University of Sussex in the UK found out that people that practice mindfulness meditation experience a greater pause between unconscious impulses and action, and are also less subject to hypnosis.

Mindfulness meditation fosters creativity

A research from Leiden University (Netherlands) demonstrates that the practice of "open monitoring" meditation (non-reactively monitoring the content of experience from moment-to-moment) has positive effects in creativity and divergent thinking. Participants who had followed the practice performed better in a task where they were asked to creatively come up with new ideas.

Body & Health

If you don't like medication, try meditation. An ounce of prevention is worth a pound of cure.

Meditation reduces risk of heart diseases and stroke

More people die of heart diseases in the world than any other illness.

In a study published in late 2012, a group of over 200 high-risk individuals was asked to either take a health education class promoting better diet and exercise or take a class on Transcendental Meditation. During the next 5 years researchers accompanying the participants found that those who took the meditation class had a 48% reduction in their overall risk of heart attack, stroke and death.

They noted that meditation "significantly reduced risk for mortality, myocardial infarction, and stroke in coronary heart disease patients. These changes were associated with lower blood pressure and psychosocial stress factors."

There are also other researches pointing out similar conclusions, about related health conditions.

Meditation affects genes that control stress and immunity

A study from Harvard Medical School demonstrates that, after practicing yoga and meditation, the individuals had improved mitochondrial energy production, consumption and resiliency. This improvement develops a higher immunity in the system and resilience to stress.

Meditation reduces blood pressure

Clinical research has demonstrated that the practice of Zen Meditation (also known as "Zazen") reduces stress and high blood pressure.

Another experiment, this time with a technique called "relaxation response", yielded similar results, with 2/3 of high blood pressure patients showing significant drops in blood pressure after 3 months of meditation, and, consequently, less need for medication. This is because relaxation results in the formation of nitric oxide, which opens up your blood vessels.

Mindfulness training decreases inflammatory disorders

A study conducted in France and Spain at the UW-Madison Waisman Centre indicates that the practice of mindfulness meditation produces a range of genetic and molecular effects on the participants. More specifically, it was noted reduced levels of pro-inflammatory genes, which in turn correlated with faster physical recovery from a stressful situation.

Mindfulness meditation decreases cellular-level inflammation

In the three studies below, the group that undertook mindfulness training had better results at preventing cellular level inflammation than the control groups.

Mindfulness practice helps prevent asthma, rheumatoid arthritis and inflammatory bowel disease

In a research conducted by neuroscientists of the University of Wisconsin-Madison, two groups of people were exposed to different methods of stress control. One of them received mindfulness training, while the other received nutritional education, exercise and music therapy. The study concluded that mindfulness techniques were more effective in relieving inflammatory symptoms than other activities that promote well-being.

Meditation and meditative prayer help treat premenstrual syndrome and menopausal symptoms

This is the conclusion of over 20 randomized control studies taken from PubMed, PsycInfo, and the Cochrane Databases, involving the techniques of Meditation, Meditative Prayer, Yoga, Relaxation Response.

yoga and mindfulness reduce stress

Mindfulness meditation reduces risk of Alzheimer's and premature death

Results from recent research, published online in the journal Brain, Behavior and Immunity, states that just 30 minutes of meditation a day not only reduces the sense of loneliness, but also reduces the risk of heart disease, depression, Alzheimer's and premature death.

Mindfulness meditation may even help treat HIV

Lymphocytes, or simply CD4 T cells, are the "brains" of the immune system, coordinating its activity when the body comes under attack. They are also the cells that are attacked by HIV, the devastating virus that causes AIDS and has infected roughly 40 million people worldwide. The virus slowly eats away at CD4 T cells, weakening the immune system. But the immune systems of HIV/AIDS patients face another enemy as well – stress, which can accelerate CD4 T cell declines. Now, researchers at UCLA report that the practice of mindfulness meditation stopped the decline of CD4 T cells in HIV-positive patients suffering from stress, slowing the progression of the disease.

Meditation may make you live longer

Telomeres are an essential part of human cells that affect how our cells age. Though the research is not conclusive yet, there is data suggesting that "some forms of meditation may have salutary effects on telomere length by reducing cognitive stress and stress arousal and increasing positive states of mind and hormonal factors that may promote telomere maintenance."

Meditation helps manage psoriasis

Psychological stress is a potent trigger of inflammation. A brief mindfulness meditation-based stress reduction intervention delivered by audiotape during ultraviolet light therapy was found to increase the resolution of psoriatic lesions in patients with psoriasis.

Health benefits of Transcendental Meditation

There is an abundance of studies around the health benefits of Transcendental Meditation (a popular modality of meditation). In a nutshell, TM is found to 4. Relationships

Meditation, though a solitary exercise, improves your personal and social relationships.

Loving-kindness meditation improves empathy and positive relationships.

Meditation enhances psychological well-beingIn Buddhist traditions we find the practice of metta, or loving-kindness meditation, where the practitioner focuses on developing a sense of benevolence and care towards all living beings. According to a study from Emory University, such exercises effectively boost one's ability to empathize with others by way of reading their facial expressions.

Another study points out that the development of positive emotions through compassion builds up several personal resources, including "a loving attitude towards oneself and others, and includes self-acceptance, social support received, and positive relations with others", as well as "feeling of competence about one's life" and includes "pathways thinking, environmental mastery, purpose in life, and ego-resilience".

Loving-kindness meditation also reduces social isolation

In a study published in the American Psychological Association, subjects that did "even just a few minutes of loving-kindness meditation increased feelings of social connection and positivity toward novel individuals, on both explicit and implicit levels. These results suggest that this easily implemented technique may help to increase positive social emotions and decrease social isolation".

Meditation increases feelings of compassion and decreases worry

After being assigned to a 9-week compassion cultivation training (CCT), individuals showed significant improvements in all three domains of compassion – compassion for others, receiving compassion from others, and self-compassion. In a similar situation, the practitioners also experienced decreased level of worry and emotional suppression.

Mindfulness meditation decreases feelings of loneliness

A study from Carnegie Mellon University indicates that mindfulness meditation training is useful in decreasing feelings of loneliness, which in turn decreases the risk for morbidity, mortality, and expression of pro-inflammatory genes.

Meditation reduces emotional eating

Scientists believe that Transcendental Meditation help manage emotional eating, which prevents obesity.

Miscellaneous

Some more interesting facts about meditation:

Saying the OM sound before a surgery helps in preparation and recovery

Meditators are more able to affect the reality around us, in a quantum level

There is also some account of mindfulness meditation improving your sex life (here, here, and here)

Reduces race and age prejudice (Sage Journals)

In a nutshell, science confirms the experience of millions of practitioners: meditation will keep you healthy, help prevent multiple diseases, make you happier, and improve your performance in basically any task, physical or mental.

How to Change Your Life in 15 Minutes a Day (Discover The Secret to Infinite Happiness)

Who else wants to be HAPPY?

Blissfully and beautifully satisfied and satiated with your lot in life.

Do you crave real contentment, joy and an unending reservoir of positive feelings that make melancholy and depression sound like words in a foreign language you don't speak?

If you read the above and are skeptical, I don't blame you. As a personal development junkie and life long self help aficionado I've been scammed, conned and taken advantage far too many times to count.

I know this sounds too good to be true......but the truth is, you DO have the ability to be happy anytime you choose. It's NOT far fetched, and it's not New Age nonsense.

The secret is simple.

In a word - the secret is meditation.

Done properly.......meditation is MAGICAL.

I'm not even sure I can tell you exactly WHY it works. There are lots of theories. Some say that it synchronizes the brain in a way that promotes positivity. Others say that it naturally increases the endorphins and neurotransmitters that regulate feelings of euphoria, bliss and beauty.

Others believe it allows us to access the wonderful "hidden" worlds around us that most folks will never experience.....simply because they've never quieted their minds for long enough to recognize that they're there.

As a matter of fact, mediation has been proven to not only make people happier, healthier, live longer and feel more connected to everything and everyone around them.....it's also well known to have tangential benefits that science is now only beginning to understand.

For example?

Increased psychic abilities (or for hard core skeptics - and increased sense of inner knowing)

Better sex

Better work performance

A more YOUTHFUL appearance (many believe that mediation

actually may BE the fountain of youth from the standpoint of slowing down, or reversing some key bio markers related to aging)

Some of these things are hard to measure....and hard to define in a lab setting.

But increased HAPPINESS is the ONE thing that almost everyone who studies mediators agrees on.

And I've YET to meet a long term mediator who has not said that they are forever changed.....and INFINITELY more happy as a result of learning to meditate.

Did you know, for example, that in many maximum security prison systems around the world, a certain type of meditative practice (called Vippassana) has reduced some of the fights, death and violence to almost ZERO?

It's true...and this has been SO effective in India and other countries in the Far East, that many are trying to implement this program in the US as well. (and the recent documentary the "Dhamma Brothers" featuring convinced murderers in Alabama featured the transformative benefits of learning to meditate in one of the worst prisons in the country)

The bottom line?

If you are sad, stuck, angry or unhappy at all.......15 minutes of mediation a day will change your life in ways that you can't imagine.

The truth is, I meditate a little longer than that about 30 minutes a day but for years, all I did was 15 minutes before work, and never looked back! If you are truly open to change and want the very BEST natural technology for making it happen, this book was written for YOU in mind. (And all you need to do is start to prove it to yourself!)

UNDERSTANDING TYPES OF MEDITATION SONGS AND THEIR WORKING PROCEDURE

Meditation is a very effective for stress relief and well-beings. Generally, meditation is a practice of concentrating only the good thoughts in our mind. It's an excellent way to keep our min calm and stress free, and having a peaceful life. It gives inspiration to a person, helps to control stress, and has numerous psychological and physical advantages. Meditation songs are considered as the most significant part of medication. There are many types of meditation songs available. Before moving on the meditation song categories, we would like to discuss about the relation between songs and meditation.

Relation between meditation and songs:

Since centuries, meditation has been practiced with background music. While meditating, music is being played from a musical source or even by hymns. Music is not bound for meditation, but it has very important role in the field of meditation. Songs make a significant ambiance for the person to concentrate. Massage therapists have been using relaxation songs since several years to create a sense of happiness and wellness during therapeutic sessions. Now you may apply the same with the convenience of your home. There are many resounding evidence which proof that meditation songs relax human's body and contribute overall well-beings and health. As people apply different types of medication techniques, there are different types of meditation songs all over the world. Now we would describe various types of meditation songs here.

Types of Meditation Music

1. Binaural Beats: Binaural beats meditative songs have become the buzz words in the field of meditation and relaxation. When binaural beats are used perfectly during medication, they can have a significant effect on mental stress and anxiety. Furthermore, they can assist in raising meditational experiences level to greater heights for the individuals who are already using other meditation techniques.

2. Monaural Beats: Monaural beats and tones are rather important in boosting your meditation practice. Usually, monaural beats or songs are some musical recordings, which are digital orchestrated and can help significantly in going deeper while meditating. If we come scientifically, these monaural beats are originated from sound wave of specific frequencies that makes a person's brain wave entrainment so as to concentrate profoundly.

3. Isochronic Tones: The effects of Isochronic tones are more powerful than binaural beats and monaural beats, and Isochronic tones are sharper sounding music than these two sounding systems.

Here it is a point to note that binaural beats, monaural beats and isochronic tones are not so melodious to listen to. To overcome this obstacle some melodious sound system like nature sounds, instrumental, chanting, the sounds of bells or chimes, etc. comes in the field of meditation.

4. Brainwave Entrainment: Usually most of the brainwave music is composed as slow tempo ambient music. It is considered as the classical orchestra music or new age meditation music. Sometimes brainwave music is embedded with background noises like some static noises which may be pink noise, brown noise, white noise,

and so on, or it may embedded with some nature sounds such as waves/ocean, birds, wind, rain, thunderstorms, etc. However it may be composed with chimes, bells, flutes, and so on. This type of sound is not only entertaining but also very effective in boosting your meditation practice.

5. Nature Sounds: Nature is regard as the best music for meditation practice. If you are interested to apply natural sounds during your meditation, you may have to go to a quite place like a forest, a garden, a hilltop, or someplace like these. Many meditation researches believe think that these natural sounds are comparable to those in a peaceful mind. Another opportunity is to buy audio CDs of nature sounds. With the most effective nature sounds these CDs have a combination of natural sounds and classical music that can incredibly enhance your concentration in meditation. Life flow provides these CDs.

6. Instrumental Music: This type of music is a suitable alternative for any kind of meditation practice. Instrumental music consists of melodious music from musical instruments such as violin, guitar, piano, chimes, sitar, flute, harp, and some other melodious sounding instruments.

7. Chanting: It is not a type of music but a method of singing in a low tone. Chanting has been applied in meditation practice for centuries many practitioners. Primordial tones may be regarded as a kind of chanting, which helps a practitioner to set his mindset right for meditation. The most famous primordial tone is 'Om' which is significantly used in India for.

Do You Know The Different Types of Meditation Techniques?

Meditation is a practice that has been around for many centuries. The different forms all have well known physical, psychological, and spiritual health benefits. Among these benefits are increased focus, relaxation, and a deeper understanding of yourself and others. But do you know the different types of meditation techniques?

Traditional Meditation

A study of the different types of meditation techniques must start with traditional forms of meditation. This form has been around for many centuries. Traditional meditation is what most people think about when they think of meditation. In this form, the meditator focuses in on a mantra, an object, a scripture, image, or a bodily function such as their breathing or heart beat or movement. When the mind wanders, the meditator brings their attention back to the focus of the meditation. This type of meditation takes a long time to master the deeper levels.

Guided Visualization

Many people have heard of this type of meditation technique. With guided visualization, the focus is on the sound of a voice as it guides you through the meditation. When listening to a recorded guided visualization, this is often accompanied by a soundtrack of some kind, usually either music (particularly the kind that is 60 beats per second or slower), rain or waterfalls, ocean waves, or a combination. The soundtrack adds to the relaxation and the guide helps you get through to deeper levels easier than if you were meditating alone.

Binaural Meditation

Based on recent scientific discoveries, this is the newest of the different types of meditation techniques. The idea behind binaural meditation is that you listen to sounds being presented to your ears in stereo.

What Are Different Types of Meditations?

There are many types of meditations that can be performed.

Different cultures and religious traditions engage in literally hundreds of types of various meditative practices. Different authorities on meditation have their own classification of the core types of meditations. I think all different types of meditations fall into three unique categories.

The first class of the meditation is the concentration meditation. This is the most popular meditation. The concentration meditation is the one that fits most closely with the general perception about what meditation should be.

In concentration meditation, you pick an object of concentration. You bring your full attention to this object of concentration. The object of concentration can be anything. It can be a physical object, specific physical sensation or your breath.

You bring your attention to the object of concentration and focus your attention on the object. Within a very short time, you will find that you have wandered away from the object of your attention. This is how your mind operates by default.

The essence of concentration meditation is that when you realize that you have wandered away from the object of your concentration, you bring yourself back to the object of attention. You do this in a nonjudgmental manner.

What is essentially happening is that you are training your brain to improve its concentration faculty. It is like flexing the muscle. You are training your mind to be more attentive and keep up attention for longer periods of time.

The second class of meditation is the awareness or insight meditation. It is also popularly known as mindfulness meditation. In a way mindfulness meditation is very similar to concentration meditation.

In mindfulness meditation you become aware of what you are doing while you are doing it. In awareness meditations your primary aim is to bring awareness to all your activities, feelings and mental states. Just as in concentration meditation you try to improve your attention by focusing on an object for extended periods, in awareness meditation you try to keep up your awareness for an extended time.

In practice you typically start with awareness of your physical self, i.e. your body. Becoming aware of your body may sound like nonsensical as you may think you are already aware of your physical body.

But that is really not the case. Because we are usually very busy with thinking, planning, ruminating and doing things. We usually just don't pay attention to our body unless it becomes sick.

Mindfulness meditation is essentially awareness training. By default we are aware of what we are doing only for a very limited set of activities. With mindfulness meditation we train our awareness to be present for more of the time.

After having practiced the awareness of the physical body, one goes on to become aware of one's thoughts. You try to become aware of the kind of thoughts your mind is engaged in. Whether those thoughts are about something that happened in the past, or it is in anticipation of what is going to happen in future.

Further on you can practice becoming aware of your feelings or emotions. This is recognizing what is your state of mind. Whether you are feeling happy, sad, angry or neutral at the current moment. You practice trying to keep up the awareness of your current emotions as moments pass by.

The third and last type of meditation is visualization meditation. Again there are many forms of visualization meditations that people practice. The main idea is to repetitively practice a particular type of visualization.

Some of the examples of visualizations involve imagining yourself getting cured of a disease, getting showered with positive energy or getting purged of negative energy.

One of the popular type of visualization meditation is called loving kindness meditation. You imagine sending loving kindness to your loved ones. You gradually expand the circle of people that you send loving kindness, the circle can potentially involve people you find difficult to get along. The visualization meditation is a form of conditioning training for your mind. By repeatedly visualizing something you condition your mind to be comfortable with that thought or idea. It may help form certain habits also.

In summary there are three high level categories of meditations:

the concentration meditation, awareness or insight meditation and the visualization meditation. The concentration meditation improves attention. The insight meditation prolongs the awareness. The visualization meditation can help with forming habits or behavior conditioning.

Beginners are advised to take it slowly; and to avoid judging their mediation skills, as this may actually increase to the already existing stress. Proper meditation takes a lot of practice and even the most experienced individual, will experience a wandering mind once in a while. The trick to efficient meditating lies, in slowly returning to your focus of concentration, as soon as the concentration is broken.

Usually, this method is done with a set of headphones so that each ear can receive different signals. The two signals resolve to a frequency that induces a meditative state in the listener. This technique can induce a meditative state that usually only comes with decades of practice using traditional meditation, even for a beginner. The biggest knock on this type of meditation is that it might seem a bit of a "cheat" because very little effort on the part of the meditator is involved.

CONCLUSION

Quite often, you will see the different types of meditation techniques combined in some way. For example, someone doing a guided visualization might also be focusing on their breathing or someone listening to a binaural meditation might also use a mantra. Most forms of meditation, whether it be the more known ones such as yoga, or an old one like tai chi, will fall into one of these main categories. Which of the different types of meditation techniques that you use is not important for most of the benefits, so find a style that you enjoy.

ABOUT THE AUTHOR

Michael Gordon was born in Dallas USA, as a child he demonstrated a strong will towards helping those around him and always showed a great level of reasoning in handling situations. He studied at the University of Southern Carolina and graduated at the age of 23. After graduation he got employed in a software development company where he worked for 5years, giving his best as a team leader by inspiring members of his team to maximize their potential and make good success.

Michael Gordon is currently the founder of his own software development company with over 38 employees on his pay roll. With his zest to ensure workplace efficiency, he engaged in the study of mediation for 2 years. He's study of mediation has helped him to write and publish several articles on the relevance of mediation and the book "21 secrets of mediation" that has gotten wildfire acceptance amongst his audience. Not leaving his company out, there is a routine performance of mediation to ensure his employees are constantly rejuvenated to achieve success.

Michael is single and resides in the northeastern part of Texas and accomplishing his dreams of being a prolific writer who can affect the lives of those around him. He enjoys biking, swimming and jogging in his leisure.